Mel Bay's Deluxe

Concertina Book

By Frank J. Converse

This book is respectfully dedicated to my life long friend, Frank Dale Quercia M.M. a fine musician-composer and member of A.S.C.A.P. and President of Honor Record Corp. I must also add that this book would never have come to fruition without his interest, efforts and encouragement.

2 3 4 5 6 7 8 9 0

PREFACE

F. CONVERSE

The Concertina was invented in England by Sir Charles Wheatstone in the year 1827. For many years it has been played "by ear" to provide music for simple affairs such as picnics, parties and square dancing. The true value and importance of this instrument has never been fully developed until recent times. All instruction books thus far available have been of the most elementary type.

It is the author's aim and expectation that the course presented, will make a significant breakthrough for the Concertina into the world of music.

This book was designed especially for you, the beginner, whether the veriest novice or the advanced player. It will provide hours of pleasure, and at the same time, advancement to the classics. Have fun!

Frank J. Converse

CONTENTS

The Concertina

20 Keys   Push-pull Type

Lefthand Key−board

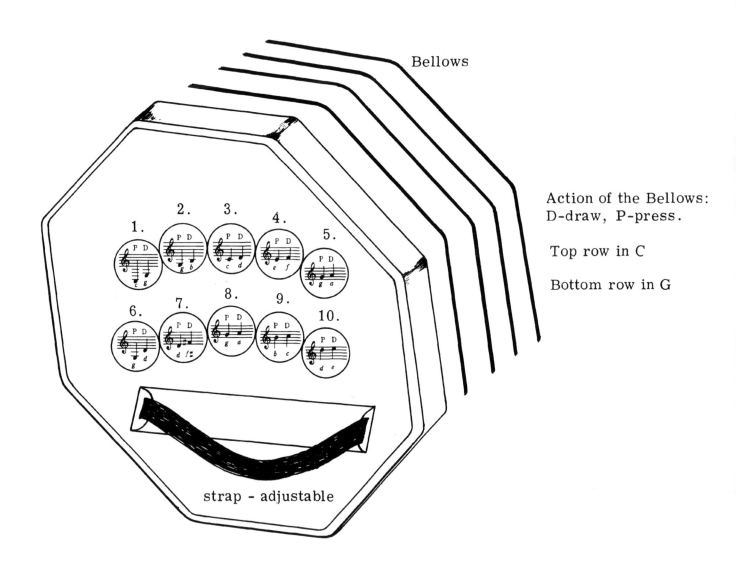

Bellows

Action of the Bellows:
D-draw, P-press.

Top row in C

Bottom row in G

strap - adjustable

Never open or close the bellows without pressing one or more keys

The Concertina

Holding the Instrument

The concertina can be played either standing or in a sitting position. The latter is prefer-
able for reading music. Sit on an armless chair with the instrument on your lap, making
certain that the air valve key is on the right side. Unfasten the bellows strap, place
fingers of each hand through the hand straps, (adjust if necessary). Thumbs remain
outside. Rest fingers on keys and notice the air valve key by your right thumb. Push air
valve key and extend the bellows by an outward movement with both arms. Still keeping
the air valve key open, close and extend the bellows a few times.

Righthand Key – board

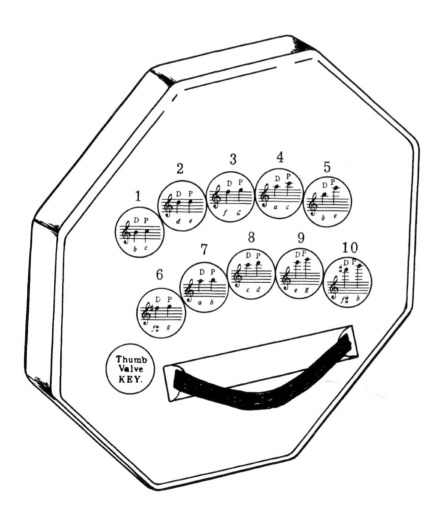

Action of the Bellows:
D-draw, P-press.

Top row in C

Bottom row in G

Never open or close the bellows without pressing one or more keys

Correct Fingering

for
Top Row Keys in the Key
of C

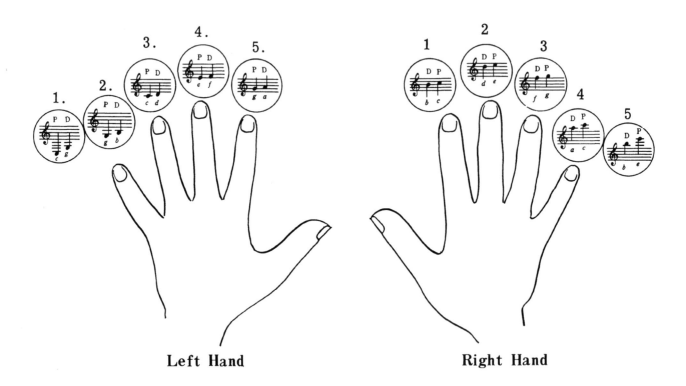

Left Hand   Right Hand

When an ex (x) is placed on top or below numbers, press or push together bellows while playing. When no mark is shown, draw or pull bellows apart while playing.

Correct Fingering

for
Bottom Row Keys in the Key
of G

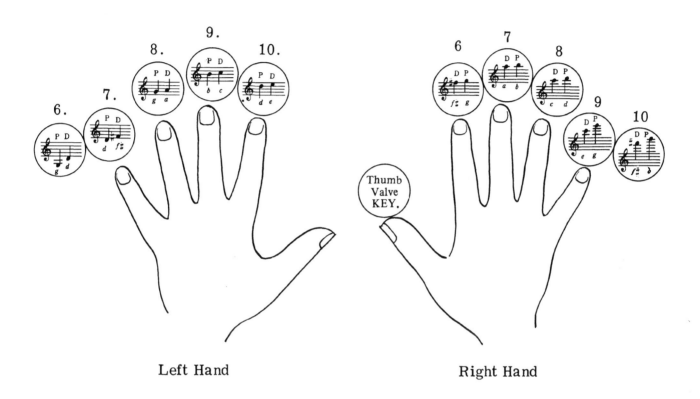

Left Hand   Right Hand

Notice that each key makes two different musical sounds, one in opening the bellows, and another in closing the bellows.

Example

After the bellows have been opened, (by means of the right hand thumb valve key,) press key No. 10. to sound the note D, while closing the bellows. Release key, depress once again to sound the note E, while opening the bellows.

Reference Chart

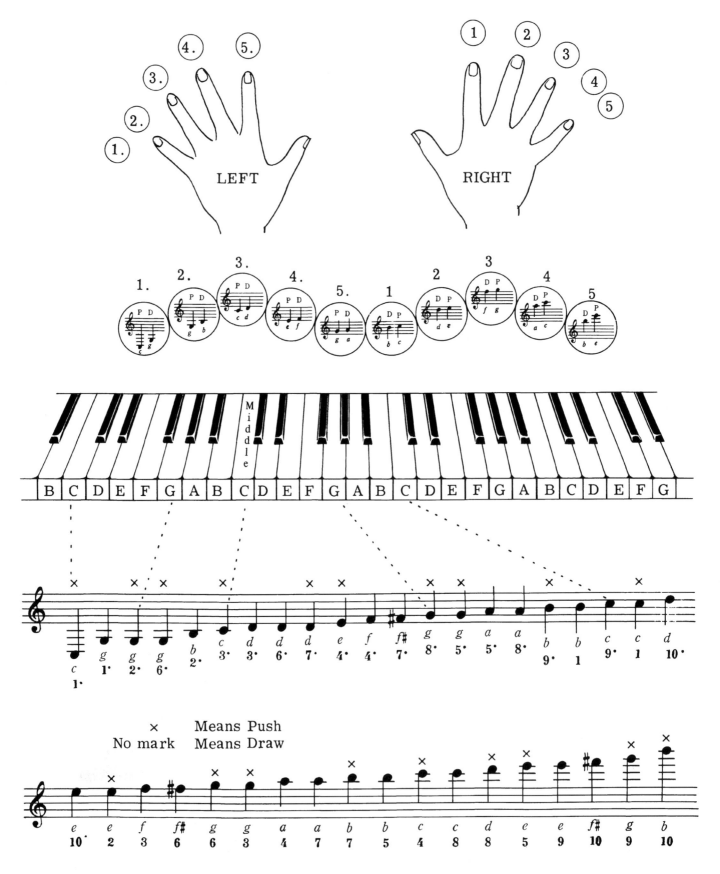

×   Means Push

No mark   Means Draw

8

Elementary Music Principles

Letter–Names of Notes

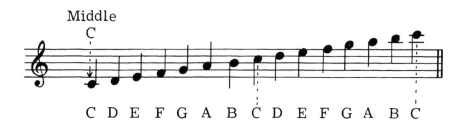

Middle C

C D E F G A B C D E F G A B C

Time Signatures

The TIME SIGNATURE placed at the beginning of a piece of music shows the number of beats in each measure of the piece. Music, like poetry, has rhythm, that is, it has accented and unaccented beats. The first beat in the measure is stressed (accented).

Here are three different TIME SIGNATURES:

The UPPER figure in the Time Signature indicates HOW MANY BEATS, or counts, in each measure - 2, 3 or 4.

The LOWER figure (4) shows that the quarter note (♩) receives one beat, or count.

(From bar line to bar line is a measure.)
(A double bar line marks the end of a piece.)

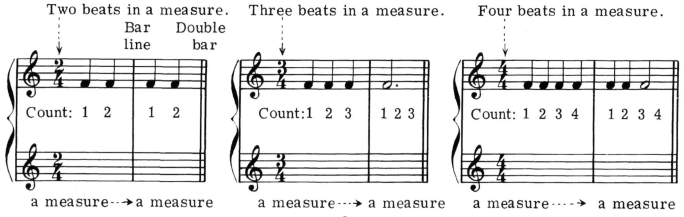

THE KEY SIGNATURE
The Flat placed on line B, just after the treble clef and after the bass clef, indicates that the note B is to be played B flat throughout the piece. This flat placed at the beginning of the piece is called the Key Signature.

TIME VALUES OF NOTES	HOW TO COUNT TIME VALUES
♩ – 1 count note (quarter-note, 1 beat)	When counting aloud, say the counts, do not sing them! Count evenly, in a short, detached, rhythmic way.
♩ – 2 count note (half-note, 2 beats)	Counting in this way, you can be sure that each note receives its exact time value.
♩· – 3 count note (dotted half note, 3 beats)	
𝅝 – 4 count note (whole-note, 4 beats)	Remember always that MELODY and RHYTHM are equally important.

The Major Scale

A SCALE is a succession of eight tones bearing letter-names in alphabetical order, the last tone having the same letter-name as the first. The figures 1, 2, 3, 4, 5, 6, 7, 8 are called the degrees of the scale.

A MAJOR SCALE is a succession of WHOLE steps and HALF steps.
The half steps occur between 3 and 4 and between 7 and 8 as follows:

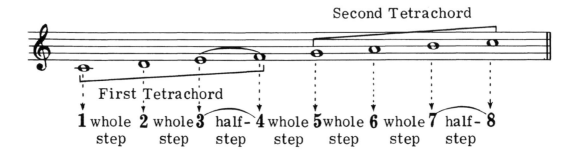

The above chart shows how a MAJOR SCALE is composed of TWO TETRACHORDS, each tetrachord separated by a WHOLE step.
Play the scale of C MAJOR as follows, using the KEYS indicated.
× Indicates to push, (close bellows.) (CB)

Scales

The following are the scales that can be played on this instrument.

Scale of C Major

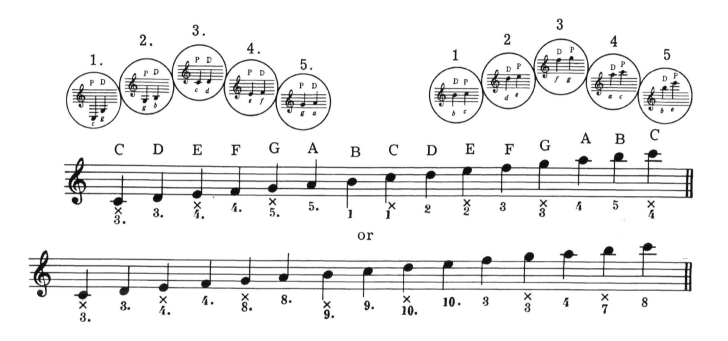

Scale of G Major

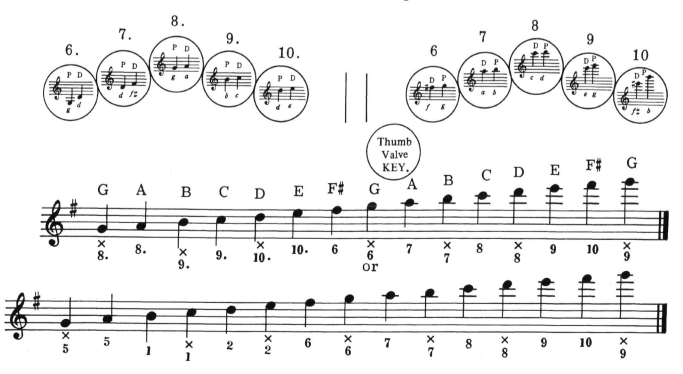

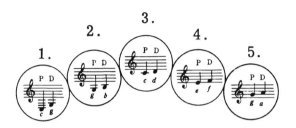

Twinkle, Twinkle Little Star

Left Hand Alone

(OB)

Twinkle	twinkle	lit-tle	star;	How I	won-der	what you	are.
C C	G G	A A	G —	F F	E E	D D	C —
3. 3.	5. 5.	5. 5.	5. —	4. 4.	4. 4.	3. 3.	3. —
× ×	× ×		×		× ×		×

Directions-
1. Open bellows by depressing the thumb value key.
2. Press key number 3. with the ring finger of your left hand.
3. Squeeze bellows to sound the note C, stop and repeat another C. you have just completed the first measure. Continue the next measure in similar fashion. - Remember, x means squeeze bellows, no mark means pull.

Up a-	bove the	world so	high,	like a	dia-mond	in the	sky!
G G	F F	E E	D —	G G	F F	E E	D —
5. 5.	4. 4.	4 4	3	5. 5.	4. 4.	4. 4.	3.
× ×		× ×		× ×		× ×	

4. To repeat a tone, lift finger and repress the same key with bellows moving in the same direction.
5. Notice that the words are in boxes, which are known as measures, in the language of music.

6. (OB) means, open bellows. (CB) means, close bellows. We must be carefull and plan ahead to conserve air in order to maintain a sufficient quantity in the bellows to play a long series of push notes.

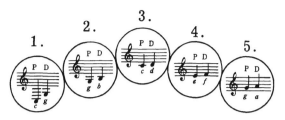

Here We Go!

Let's play some of these familiar melodies.

This Old Man
Left Hand Alone

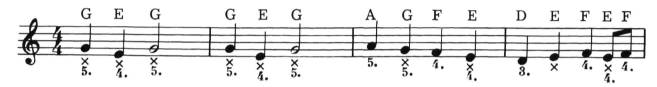

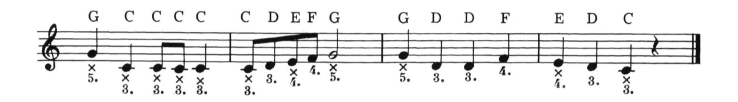

Carnival in Venice
Left Hand Alone

13

Old MacDonald

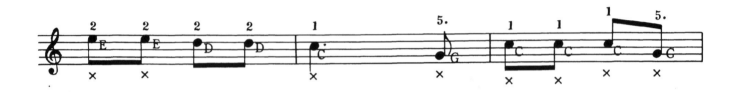

Shoo Fly

Oh Where has My Little Dog Gone
Left Hand Alone

America
Right Hand Alone

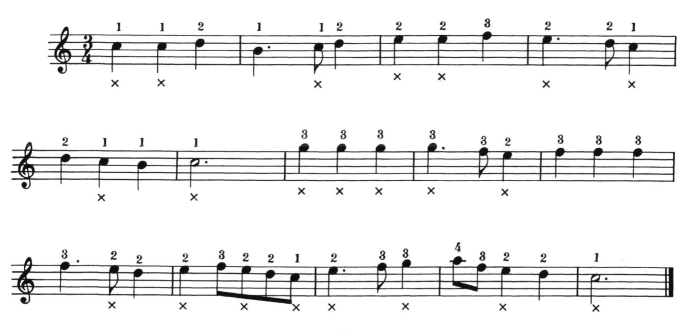

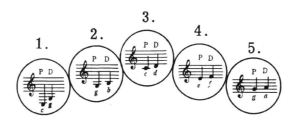

Hot Cross Buns
Left Hand Only

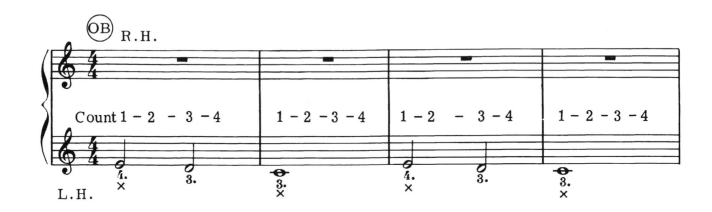

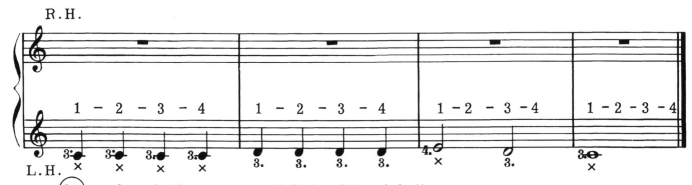

(OB) = Open bellows, press right hand thumb button.

(CB) = Close bellows, press right hand thumb button.

R.H.= Right hand.

L.H.= Left hand.

×　= Press bellows

No mark = Draw bellows

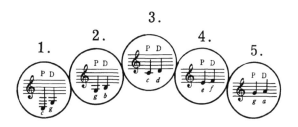

Left Hand

Merrily We Roll Along

Traditional

Moderato

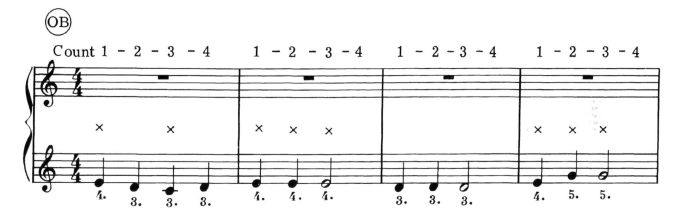

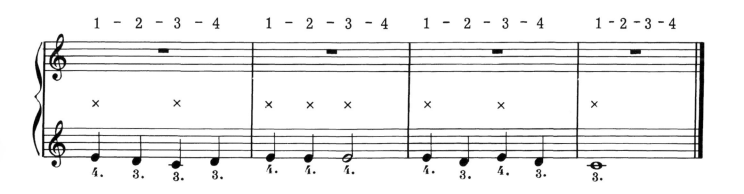

Some Folks Do

Stephen Foster
Arr. by F. Converse

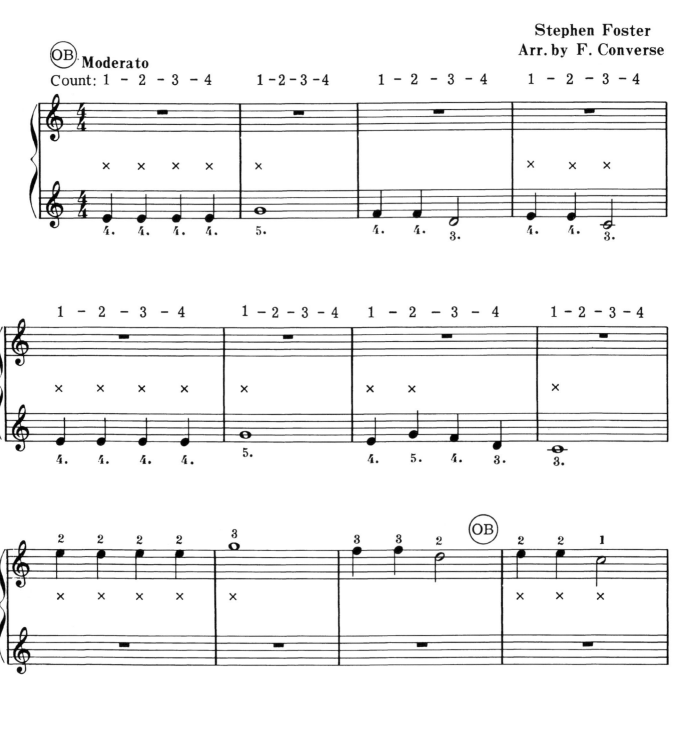

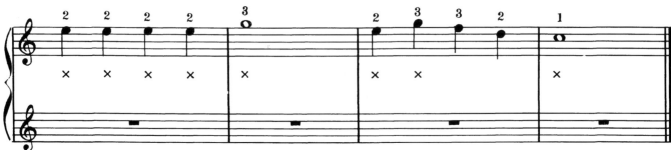

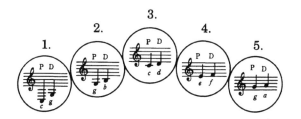

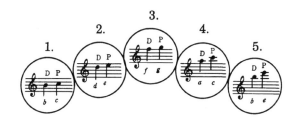

Song of the Volga Boatmen

Russian Song
Arr. by F. Converse

Andante

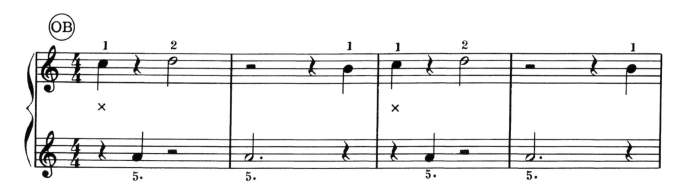

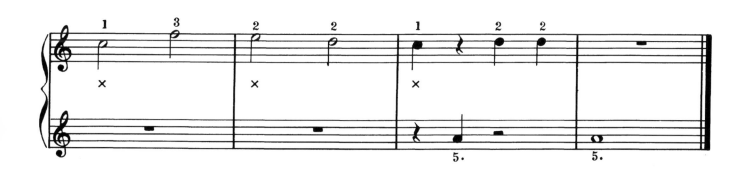

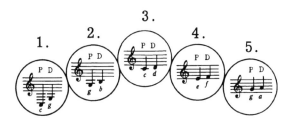

You are Always in My Heart

Traditional

Waltz tempo

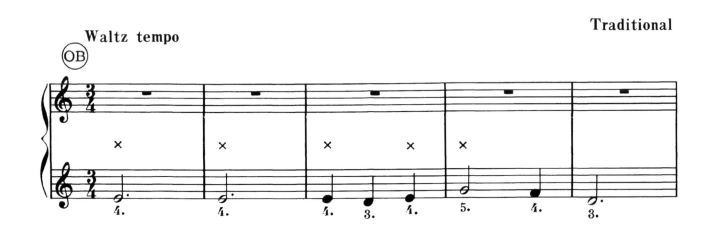

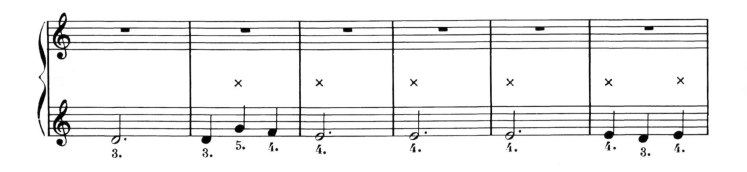

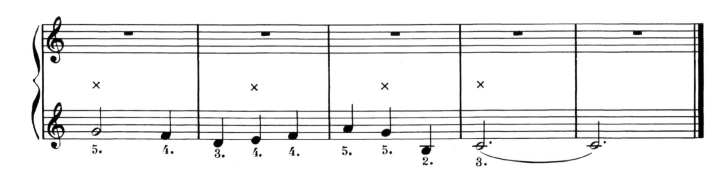

20

Good Night Ladies

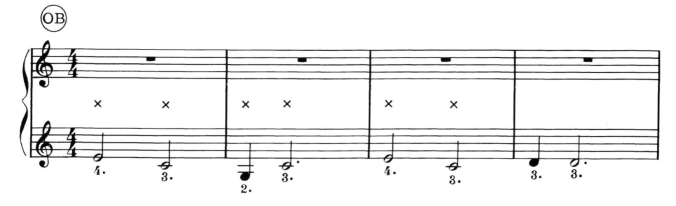

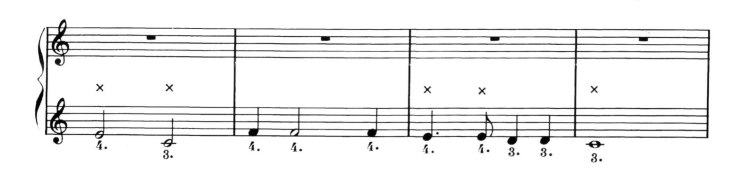

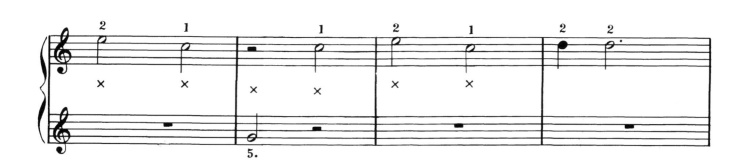

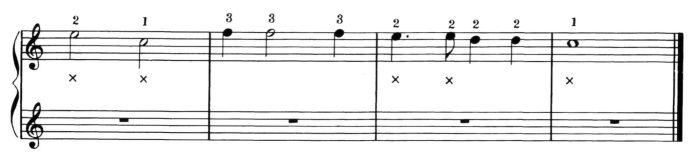

Polly Wolly Doodle

College Song

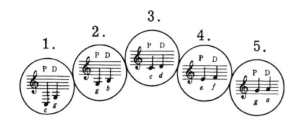

Left Hand

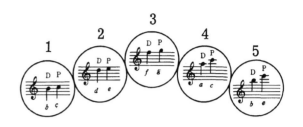

Right Hand

Rock - a - bye Baby

Traditional

Moderato

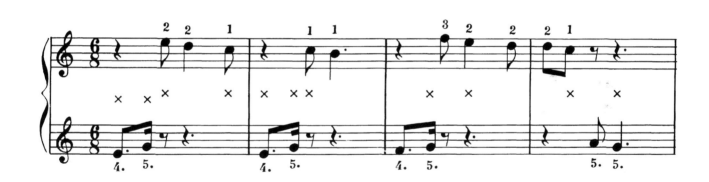

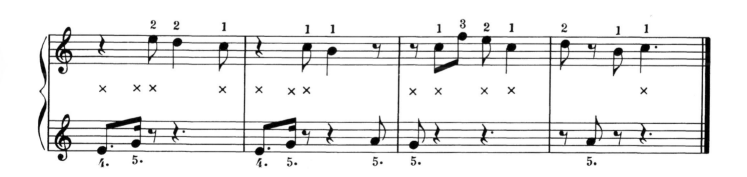

23

Aloha Oe

Queen Lydia Liliuokalani
Arr. by F. Converse

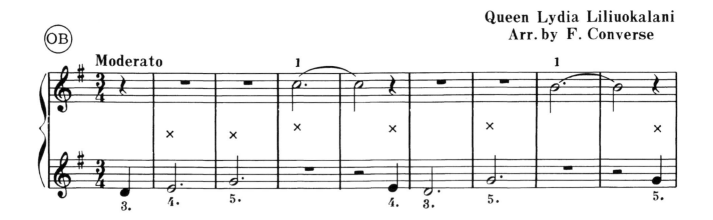

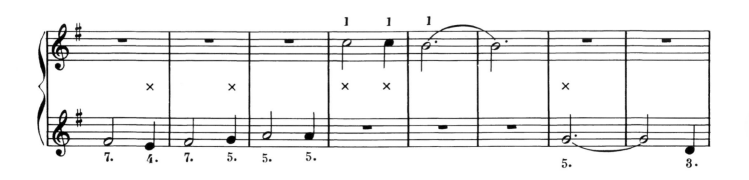

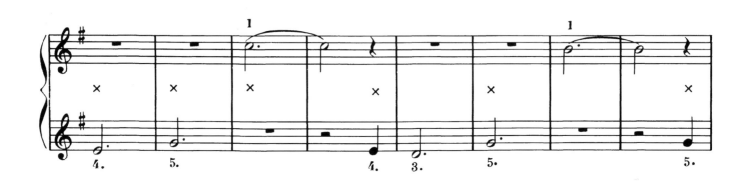

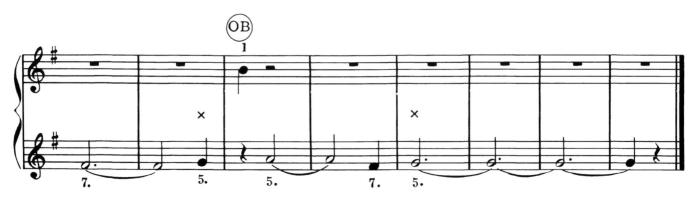

Humoreske

Dvorak
Arr. by F. Converse

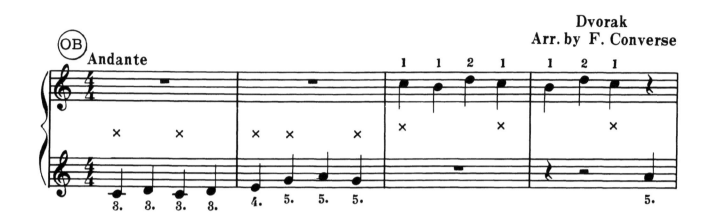

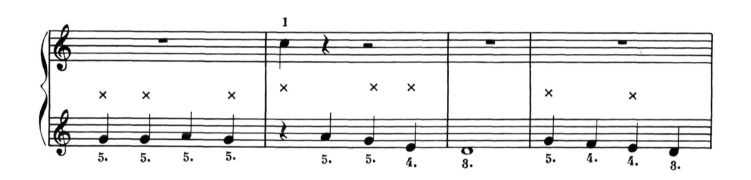

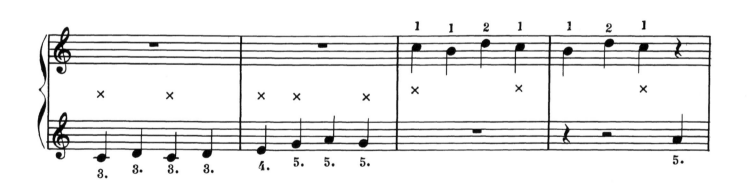

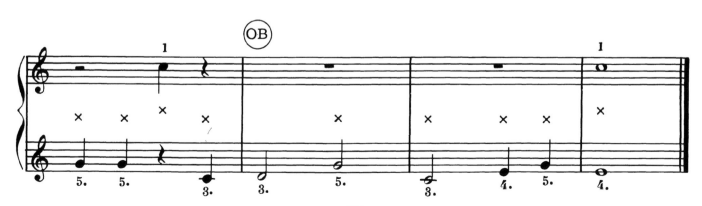

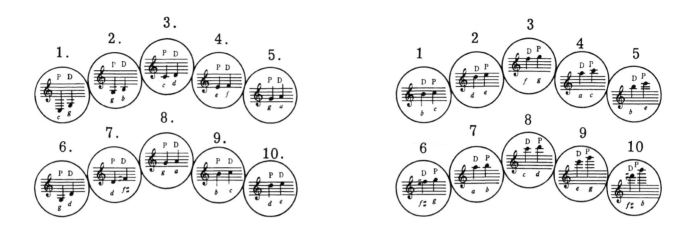

The Wishing Star

German Folk Tune

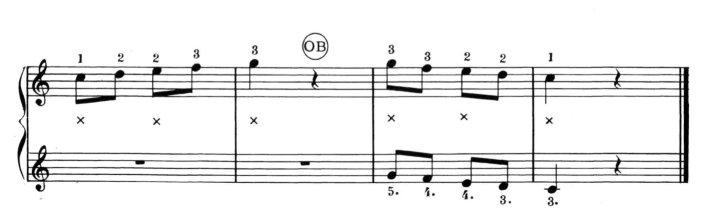

Oh, My Darling Clementine

In the cav-ern, in a can-yon Ex-ca-vat-ing for a mine, Dwelt a
min-er, for-ty-nin-er, And his daugh-ter Clem-en-tine. Oh my

Chorus

dar-ling, oh my dar-ling, Oh my dar-ling Clem en-tine; You are
lost and gone for-ev-er, Dread-ful sor-ry Clem-en-tine

I've been Workin' on the Railroad

I've been Work-in' on the rail-road, All the live-long day,
I've been Work-in' on the rail-road, just to pass the time a-way.
Don't you hear the whis-tle blow-in' Rise up so ear-ly in the morn;
Don't you hear the capt'-n shout — 'in Din-ah, blow that horn.

27

I Love You Truly

Carrie Jacobs-Bond

28

La Francesa

Traditional

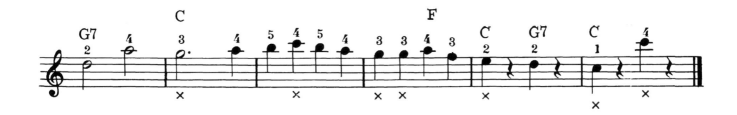

She'll be Comin' Round the Mountain

Aura Lee

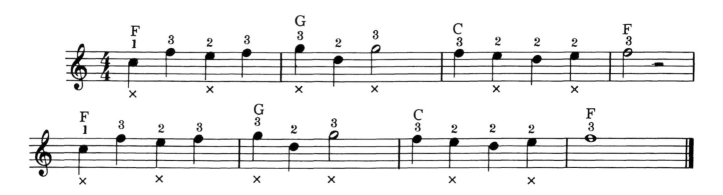

Ode to Joy

Beethoven

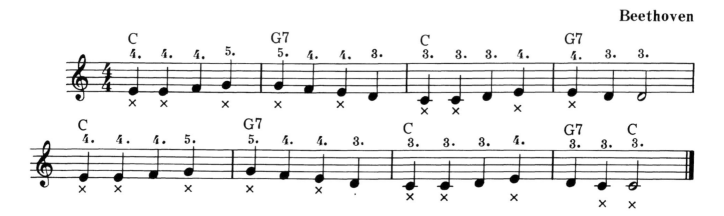

Hi − Lee, Hi − Lo

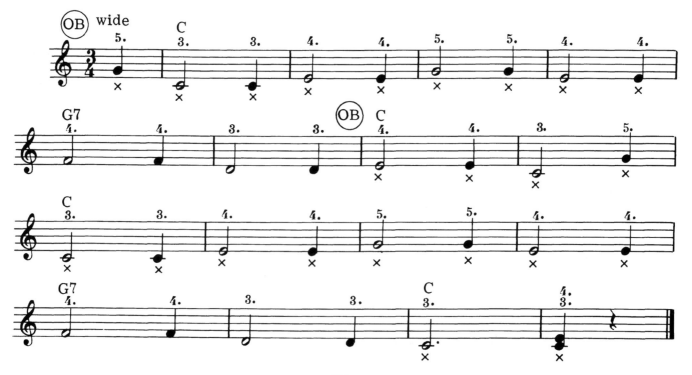

Irish Reel

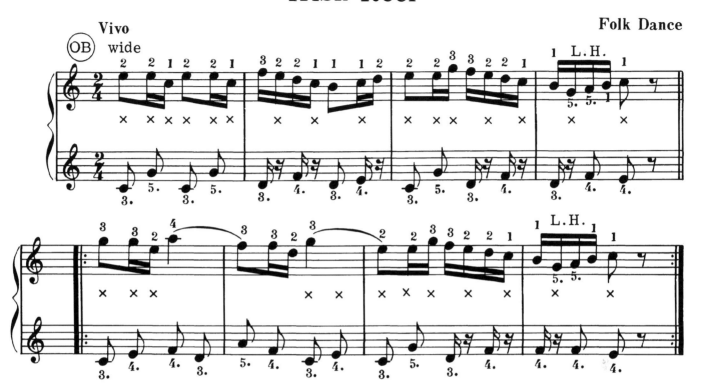

Gary Owen

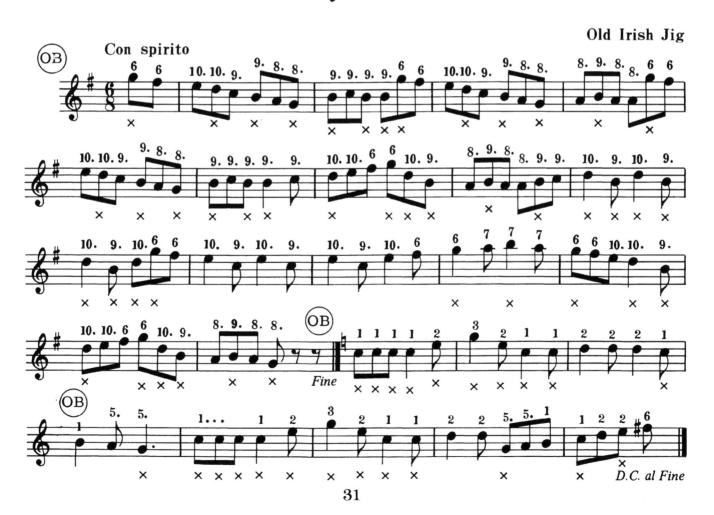

Country Gardens

Traditional

32

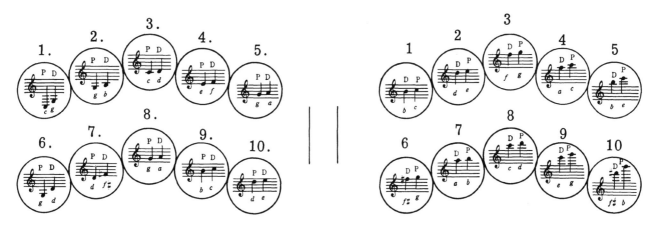

Home on the Range

Moderato

Folk Song

Oh give me a home where the buf - fa - lo roam, Where the

deer and the an - te - lope play, _____ Where

nev - er is heard a dis - cour - ag - ing word and the

skies are not cloud - y all day, _____

Home, home on the range, _____ Where the

deer and the an - te - lope play; _____ Where

nev - er is heard a dis - cour - ag - ing word and the

skies are not cloud - y all day. _____

When You Were Sweet Sixteen

Janies Thorton

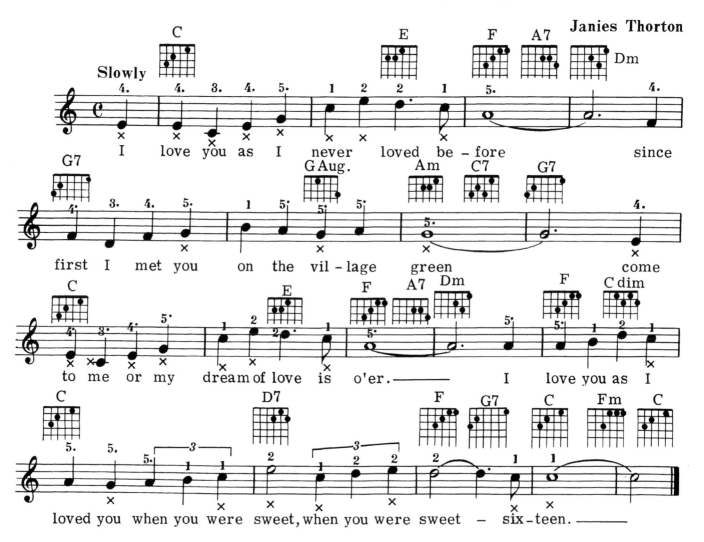

I love you as I never loved be - fore since

first I met you on the vil - lage green come

to me or my dream of love is o'er.———— I love you as I

loved you when you were sweet, when you were sweet - six-teen.————

Bring Back My Bonnie to Me

Billy Boy

Old English Song

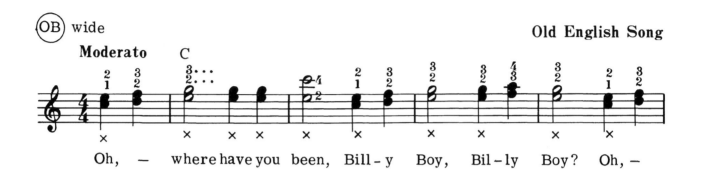

Oh, — where have you been, Bill - y Boy, Bil - ly Boy? Oh, —

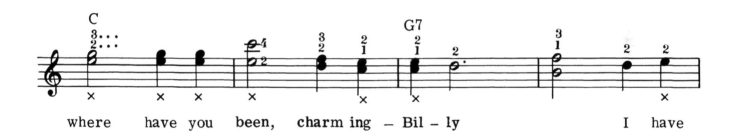

where have you been, charm ing — Bil - ly I have

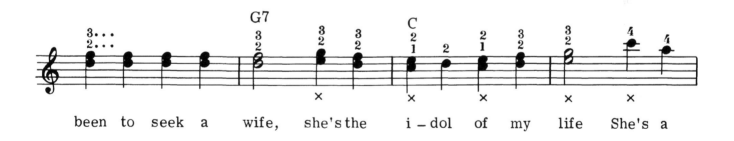

been to seek a wife, she's the i - dol of my life She's a

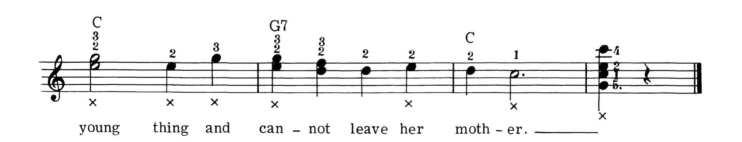

young thing and can - not leave her moth - er. _____

Burning Charlotte Town

Traditional

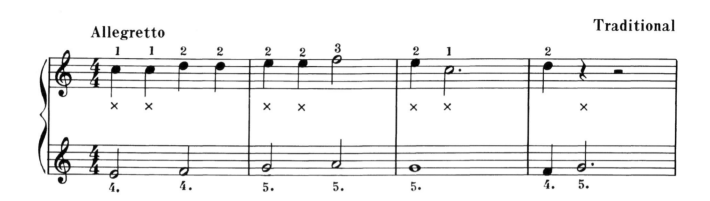

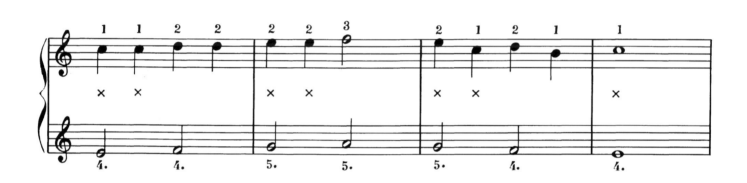

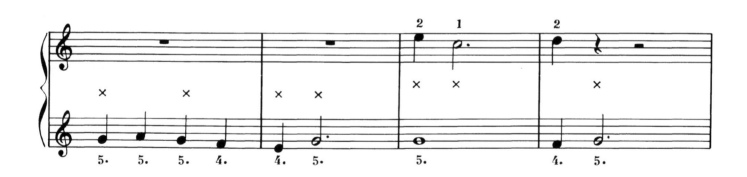

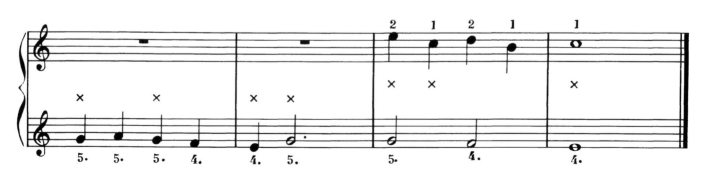

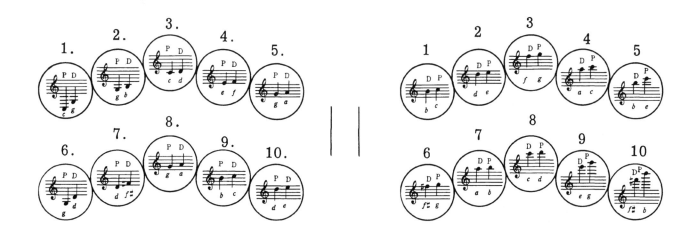

Sur le pont D'avignon

French Folk Song
Arr. by F. Converse

Are You Sleeping?

French Folk Song
Arr. by F. Converse

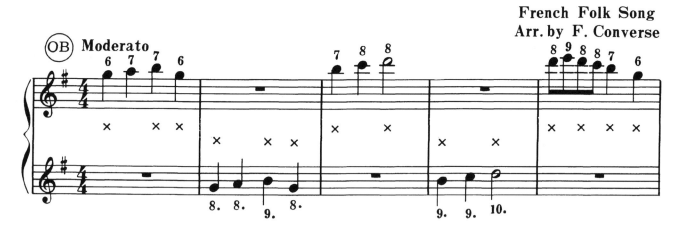

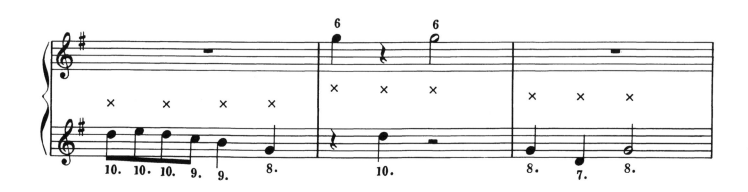

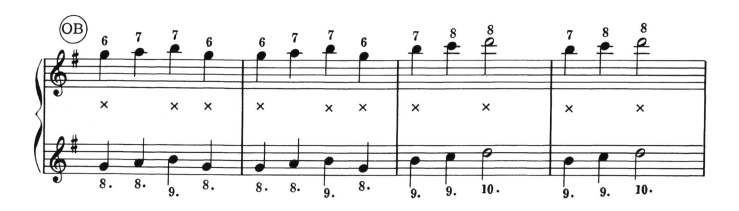

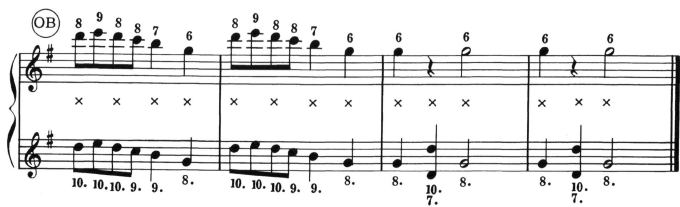

Michael, Row the Boat Ashore

Traditional
Arr. by F. Converse

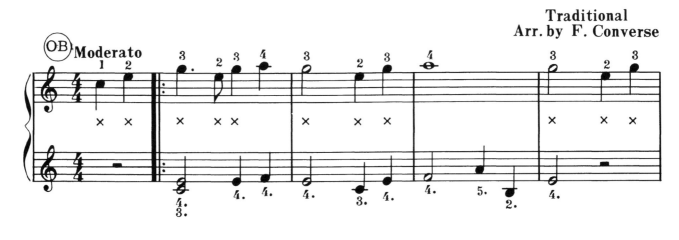

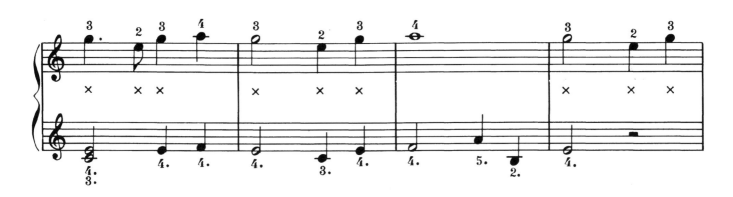

Play once through to repeat sign :‖ skip 1st ending, the second time through, play 2nd ending.

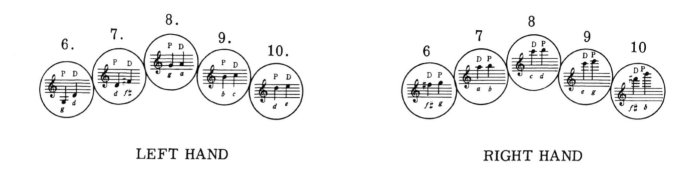

LEFT HAND   RIGHT HAND

Bottom Row Key of G

The Farmer in the Dell

Traditional

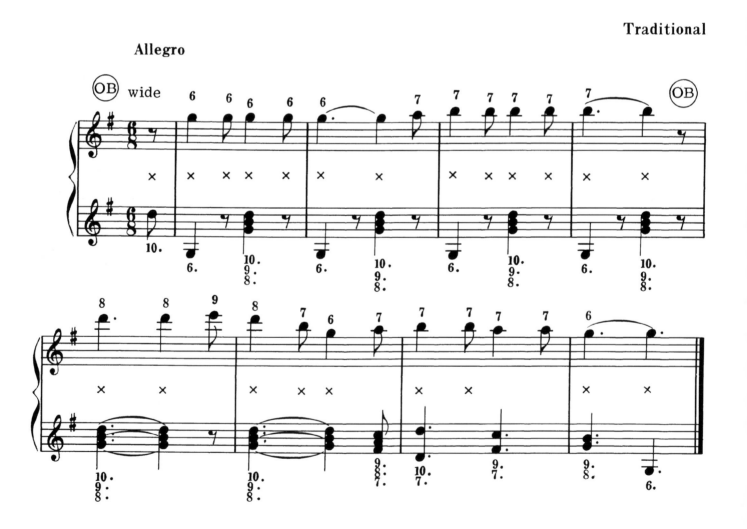

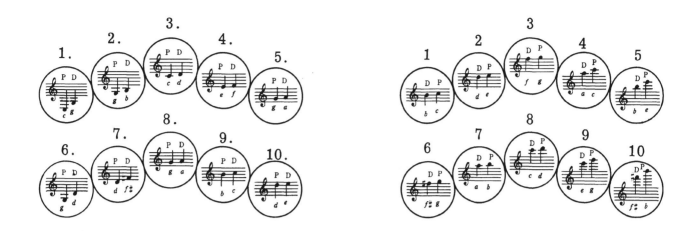

At Pierrot's Door

French Folk Song
Arr. by F. Converse

The Emperor Waltz

Strauss
Arr. by F. Converse

42

Sonatina

Beethoven
Arr. by F. Converse

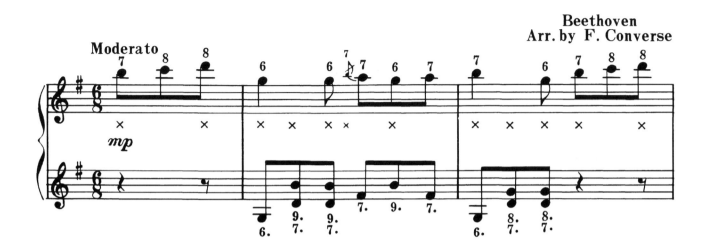

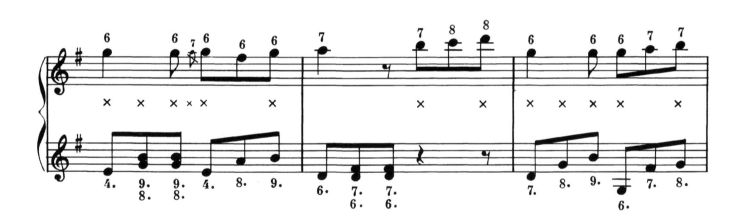

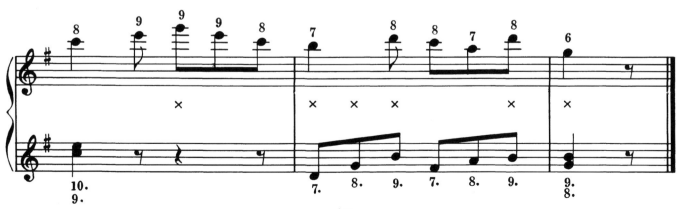

Rondalla

R.H. Plays 8 Notes Higher

E. Grados
Arr. by F. Converse

Wedding March

R. Wagner
Arr. by F. Converse

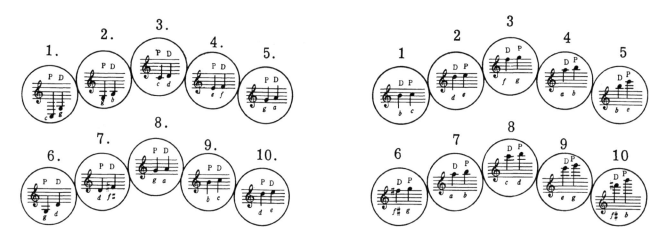

Musetta's Waltz

G. Puccini
Arr. by F. Converse

46

Lullaby

J. Brahms
Arr. by F. Converse

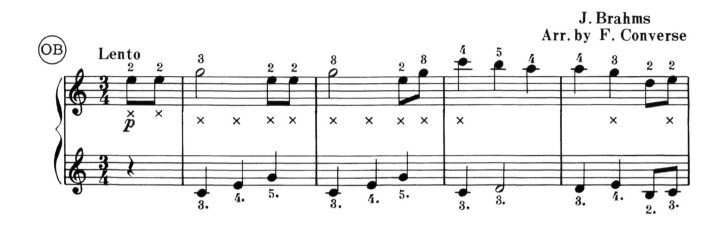

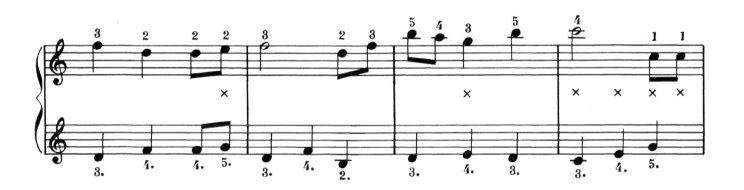

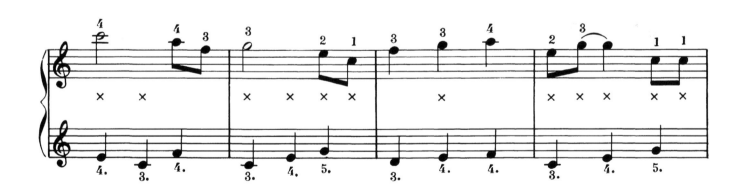

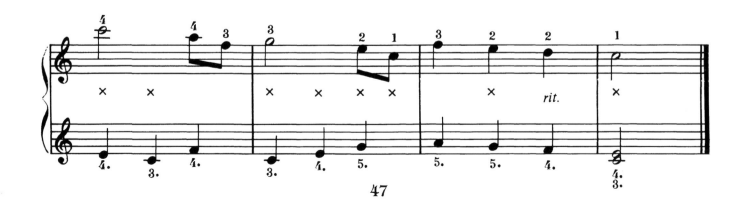

Caro Mio Ben
(Thou, All My Bliss)

G. Giordani
Arr. by F. Converse

La Sorella

Gallini

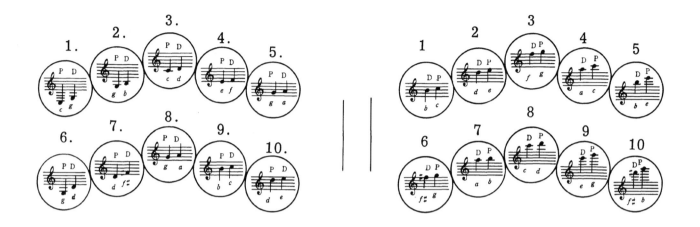

Concertina Concerto

Mozart
Arr. by F. Converse

50

51

Swallows in Flight

Traditional
Arr. by F. Converse